ROYAL COURT

The Royal Court Theatre presents

A MIRACLE

by **Molly Davies**

First performance at the Royal Court Jerwood Theatre Upstairs,
Sloane Square, London on 27th February 2009

The Young Writers Festival is supported by
John Lyon's Charity
with additional funding from
the **John Thaw Foundation** and
the **D'Oyly Carte Charitable Trust**

28 March – 2 May
ROYAL COURT
tusk tusk
by polly stenham
As hilarious as it is heart-breaking *Tusk Tusk* is a tale of Family ties. This is Polly Stenham's second play following her award-winning debut *That Face*.
Supported by
JERWOOD
NEW PLAYWRIGHTS
020 7565 5000 Tickets £15 (£10 Mondays and concessions)
www.royalcourttheatre.com
ARTS COUNCIL ENGLAND

A MIRACLE

by **Molly Davies**

Cast in order of appearance

VAL **Sorcha Cusack**
AMY **Kate O'Flynn**
GARY **Russell Tovey**
ROB **Gerard Horan**

Director **Lyndsey Turner**
Designer **Patrick Burnier**
Lighting Designer **Nicki Brown**
Sound Designer **David McSeveney**
Assistant Director **Keziah Serreau**
Casting Director **Amy Ball**
Production Manager **Tariq Rifaat**
Stage Managers **Martha Mamo, Ruth Murfitt**
Costume Supervisor **Jackie Orton**

THE COMPANY

MOLLY DAVIES (Writer)

Molly won the Westminster Prize for her 10 minute play No Fairy Stories (Soho Theatre). For young audiences, she has written Day One (National Youth Theatre), The Best Team Since the A-Team (Southwark Playhouse) and My Days (Soho/Company of Angels). She is a graduate of the Royal Court Young Writers Programme. A Miracle is her first full-length play.

Molly was born in Norfolk.

PATRICK BURNIER (Designer)

THEATRE INCLUDES: The Brothers Size (Young Vic/UK Tour); Reverence (Southwark Playhouse); Le Vaillant Petit Tailleur (Swiss Tour); In The Jungle of The Cities (RADA); The Balcony (Théâtre de l'Athénée, Paris); The Bacchae (Théâtre du Moulin-Neuf, Switzerland).

DANCE INCLUDES: Entity: A Diptych (Sadler's Wells); Shore (Bamburgh Castle); Concert en 5 Actes (Théâtre des Terreaux, Switzerland).

AWARDS INCLUDE: 2005 Linbury Biennial Prize for Theatre Design.

NICKI BROWN (Lighting Designer)

FOR THE ROYAL COURT: Contractions; Paradise Regained; Fear & Misery and War & Peace; Gone Too Far! (JTU), 93.2FM (& UK tour).

OTHER THEATRE INCLUDES: The Exquisite Corpse (Wales Millennium Centre & Edinburgh); Ours (Finborough); The Elephant Man (Union and Brazilian tour); Hamlet (UK and Beirut); By Parties Unknown (Site specific, Sincera Productions); Splendour (Cobden); Dr Faustus (Etcetera); A Million Hearts for Mosley (MacOwan).

Nicki is Lighting Deputy at the Royal Court.

SORCHA CUSACK (Val)

FOR THE ROYAL COURT: Three Sisters.

OTHER THEATRE INCLUDES: The 5 Wives of Maurice Pinder (National); Romeo & Juliet, King John (RSC); Sunday Bloody Sunday (Tricycle); By the Bog of Cats (Wyndhams Theatre, West End); Anthony and Cleopatra, The Roaring Girl (RSC); The Vagina Monologues (No. 1 Tour); A View from the Bridge (Centreline); Feast of Snails (Lyric Theatre, West End); Peer Gynt, The Playboy of the Western World (National); Baglady (Traverse/Lyric Theatre); Give Me Your Answer, Do!, Carthaginians (Hampstead); The Plough and the Stars, The Playboy of the Western World (West Yorkshire Playhouse); Dancing at Lughnasa (Phoenix & Garrick); Les Liaisons Dangereuses (Gate, Dublin); Three Sisters (Rostet); The Plough and the Stars, Much Ado About Nothing, A Doll's House (Abbey); Freedom of the City (Abbey/Lincoln Centre, New York); Lower Depths, The Odd Women, The Cherry Orchard (Royal Exchange); Duchess of Malfi (Royal Exchange/Roundhouse).

TELEVISION INCLUDES: Dalziel and Pascoe: Glory Days, Judge John Deed, Inspector Lynley, Silent Witness, Pulling Moves, Playing the Field, Eureka Street, Plastic Man, Casualty, Poirot, Maigret, Inspector Morse, Permanent Red, August Saturday, The Real Charlotte, The Bill, Ulysses, Private Affairs, Married Love, Napoleon and Love, Jane Eyre.

FILM INCLUDES: Middletown, Past Present Future Imperfect, Dogma 3: Tamed, One of the Hollywood 10, Snatch, Sinful Davey, Angel, A Hitch in Time,

GERARD HORAN (Rob)

FOR THE ROYAL COURT: The Weir, A Whistle in the Dark, Saved/The Pope's Wedding, Built on Sand, Up to the Sun, Downfall, Rat in the Skull.

OTHER THEATRE INCLUDES: Rat in the Skull (Public Theatre New York); Man and Superman (Citizens Glasgow); Public Enemy, Look Back in Anger, A Midsummer Night's Dream, King Lear, Coriolanus (Renaissance); The Plough and the Stars (West Yorkshire Playhouse); Blue Remembered Hills (National Theatre); Richard III (Sheffield Crucible); Insignificance (Sheffield Lyceum).

TELEVISION INCLUDES; Lark Rise to Candleford, Kingdom, Doctor Who, The Green Green Grass, Banglatown Banquet, The Chatterley Affair, Dalziel and Pascoe, Doc Martin, Murder in Rome, Tom Brown's Schooldays, Tamworth Two, Dr Jekyll and Mr Hyde, NCS-Manhunt, Hot Money, Never Never, Sleeper, This is Personal, Harbour Lights, Wycliffe, The Ice House, Beast in Man, Look Back in Anger, Shoot to Kill, Poirot, The Grass Arena, The Singing Detective, London's Burning.

FILM INCLUDES: The Bank Job, Breaking and Entering, As You Like It, Oliver Twist, Bright Young Things, Nicholas Nickleby, The Last Great Wilderness, Les Miserables, In the Bleak Midwinter, Immortal Beloved, Frankenstein, Midnight Movie, Much Ado About Nothing, Chicago Joe and the Show Girl, Hidden City, Sammy and Rosie Get Laid, My Beautiful Laundrette.

DAVID McSEVENEY (Sound Designer)

FOR THE ROYAL COURT: Shades, The Stone, The Girlfriend Experience (& Theatre Royal Plymouth), Contractions, Fear &Misery/War & Peace.

OTHER THEATRE INCLUDES: Gaslight (Old Vic); Charley's Aunt, An Hour and a Half Late (Theatre Royal Bath); A Passage to India, After Mrs Rochester, Madame Bovary (Shared Experience); Men Should Weep, Rookery Nook (Oxford Stage Company); Othello (Southwark Playhouse).

AS ASSISTANT DESIGNER: The Permanent Way (Out of Joint); My Brilliant Divorce, Auntie and Me (West End); Accidental Death of an Anarchist (Donmar).

ORIGINAL MUSIC: The BFG (Secret Theatre Productions).

David is Sound Deputy at the Royal Court.

KATE O'FLYNN (Amy)

THEATRE INCLUDES: See How They Run, The Children's Hour (Manchester Royal Exchange).

TELEVISION INCLUDES: Kingdom, The Palace, Trial & Retribution, Heartbeat.

FILM INCLUDES: Happy-Go-Lucky.

AWARDS INCLUDE: 2008 TMA Award Best Supporting Performance, 2008 MEN Award for Best Newcomer.

RUSSELL TOVEY (Gary)

FOR THE ROYAL COURT: Plasticine.

OTHER THEATRE INCLUDES: The Sea (Theatre Royal Haymarket); A Respectable Wedding (Young Vic), The History Boys (National/Broadway); Tintin (Barbican/Young Vic); The Laramie Project (Sound); His Dark Materials, His Girl Friday, Henry V, Howard Katz (National); The Recruiting Officer (Chichester).

TELEVISION INCLUDES: Miss Marple: Murder is Easy, Being Human, Little Dorrit, Mutual Friends, Ashes to Ashes, Doctor Who, Annually Retentive, Gavin & Stacey, My Family & Other Animals, Messiah: The Harrowing, Servants, Silent Witness, Ultimate Force, NCS, Poirot: Evil Under the Sun, Suffocation, Hope & Glory, Anchor Me, Mrs Bradley Mysteries.

FILM INCLUDES: The History Boys, The Emperor's New Clothes.

LYNDSEY TURNER (Director)

FOR THE ROYAL COURT: Contractions.

OTHER THEATRE INCLUDES: The Lesson (Arcola); Contractions, Still Breathing, What's Their Life Got, Paris Hilton, The Good Guy Gets The Girl, Hymn (Theatre 503); Halo Boy and the Village of Death (Edinburgh Festival Fringe); Antony and Cleopatra, Twelve Angry Men, Arabian Nights, The Servant to Two Masters (MFH).

AS ASSISTANT DIRECTOR FOR THE ROYAL COURT: The City, The Vertical Hour, Rhinoceros, Drunk Enough to Say I Love You?, Krapp's Last Tape, The Winterling.

THE ENGLISH STAGE COMPANY AT THE ROYAL COURT

'For me the theatre is really a religion or way of life. You must decide what you feel the world is about and what you want to say about it, so that everything in the theatre you work in is saying the same thing ... A theatre must have a recognisable attitude. It will have one, whether you like it or not.'

George Devine, first artistic director of the English Stage Company: notes for an unwritten book.

photo: Stephen Cummiskey

As Britain's leading national company dedicated to new work, the Royal Court Theatre produces new plays of the highest quality, working with writers from all backgrounds, and addressing the problems and possibilities of our time.

"The Royal Court has been at the centre of British cultural life for the past 50 years, an engine room for new writing and constantly transforming the theatrical culture." Stephen Daldry

Since its foundation in 1956, the Royal Court has presented premieres by almost every leading contemporary British playwright, from John Osborne's *Look Back in Anger* to Caryl Churchill's *A Number* and Tom Stoppard's *Rock 'n' Roll*. Just some of the other writers to have chosen the Royal Court to premiere their work include Edward Albee, John Arden, Richard Bean, Samuel Beckett, Edward Bond, Jez Butterworth, Martin Crimp, Ariel Dorfman, Christopher Hampton, David Hare, Eugène Ionesco, Ann Jellicoe, Terry Johnson, Sarah Kane, David Mamet, Martin McDonagh, Conor McPherson, Joe Penhall, Mark Ravenhill, Simon Stephens, Wole Soyinka, Polly Stenham, David Storey, Debbie Tucker Green, Arnold Wesker and Roy Williams.

"It is risky to miss a production there." Financial Times

In addition to its full-scale productions, the Royal Court also facilitates international work at a grass roots level, developing exchanges which bring young writers to Britain and sending British writers, actors and directors to work with artists around the world. The research and play development arm of the Royal Court Theatre, The Studio, finds the most exciting and diverse range of new voices in the UK. The Studio runs playwriting groups including the Young Writers Programme, Critical Mass for black, Asian and minority ethnic writers and the bi-annual Young Writers Festival. For further information, go to www.royalcourttheatre.com/ywp

"Yes, the Royal Court is on a roll. Yes, Dominic Cooke has just the genius and kick that this venue needs... It's fist-bitingly exciting." Independent

PROGRAMME SUPPORTERS

The Royal Court (English Stage Company Ltd) receives its principal funding from Arts Council England, London. It is also supported financially by a wide range of private companies, charitable and public bodies, and earns the remainder of its income from the box office and its own trading activities.

The Genesis Foundation supports the Royal Court's work with International Playwrights.

The Jerwood Charitable Foundation supports new plays by new playwrights through the Jerwood New Playwrights series.

The Artistic Director's Chair is supported by a lead grant from The Peter Jay Sharp Foundation, contributing to the activities of the Artistic Director's office. Over the past ten years the BBC has supported the Gerald Chapman Fund for directors.

ROYAL COURT DEVELOPMENT ADVOCATES
John Ayton
Elizabeth Bandeen
Anthony Burton
Sindy Caplan
Cas Donald
Allie Esiri
Celeste Fenichel
Stephen Marquardt
Emma Marsh (Vice Chair)
Mark Robinson
William Russell (Chair)
David Winterfeldt

PUBLIC FUNDING
Arts Council England, London
British Council
London Challenge

CHARITABLE DONATIONS
American Friends of the Royal Court Theatre
Anthony Burton
Gerald Chapman Fund
The Sidney & Elizabeth Corob Charitable Trust
Cowley Charitable Trust
Credit Suisse First Boston Foundation *
The Edmond de Rothschild Foundation*
Do Well Foundation Ltd*
The D'Oyly Carte Charitable Trust
Esmée Fairbairn Foundation
The Edwin Fox Foundation
Francis Finlay*
Frederick Loewe Foundation *
The Garfield Weston Foundation
Genesis Foundation
Haberdashers' Company
Jerwood Charitable Foundation
John Thaw Foundation
Kudos Film and Televisoin
Lynn Foundation
John Lyon's Charity

The Laura Pels Foundation*
The Martin Bowley Charitable Trust
The Patchwork Charitable Foundation*
Paul Hamlyn Foundation
Quercus Charitable Trust
Jerome Robbins Foundation*
Rose Foundation
The Rosenkranz Foundation*
The Royal Victoria Hall Foundation
The Peter Jay Sharp Foundation*
Sobell Foundation
Wates Foundation

CORPORATE SUPPORTERS & SPONSORS
BBC
Hugo Boss
Links of London
Pemberton Greenish

BUSINESS BENEFACTORS & MEMBERS
Grey London
Lazard
Merrill Lynch
Vanity Fair

INDIVIDUAL SUPPORTERS

ICE-BREAKERS
Act IV
Anonymous
Ossi & Paul Burger
Mrs Helena Butler
Cynthia Corbett
Shantelle David
Charlotte & Nick Fraser
Mark & Rebecca Goldbart
Linda Grosse
Mr & Mrs Tim Harvey-Samuel
The David Hyman Charitable Trust
David Lanch
Colette & Peter Levy
Watcyn Lewis

David Marks
Nicola McFarland
Janet & Michael Orr
Pauline Pinder
Mr & Mrs William Poeton
The Really Useful Group
Lois Sieff OBE
Gail Steele
Nick & Louise Steidl

GROUND-BREAKERS
Anonymous
Moira Andreae
Jane Attias*
Elizabeth & Adam Bandeen
Philip Blackwell
Mrs D H Brett
Sindy & Jonathan Caplan
Mr & Mrs Gavin Casey
Carole & Neville Conrad
Clyde Cooper
Andrew & Amanda Cryer
Robyn M Durie
Hugo Eddis
Mrs Margaret Exley CBE
Robert & Sarah Fairbairn
Celeste & Peter Fenichel
Andrew & Jane Fenwick
Ginny Finegold
Wendy Fisher
Hugh & Henri Fitzwilliam-Lay
Joachim Fleury
John Garfield
Lydia & Manfred Gorvy
Richard & Marcia Grand*
Reade and Elizabeth Griffith
Nick & Catherine Hanbury-Williams
Sam & Caroline Haubold
Mr & Mrs J Hewett
Nicholas Josefowitz
David P Kaskel & Christopher A Teano
Peter & Maria Kellner*
Mrs Joan Kingsley & Mr Philip Kingsley
Mr & Mrs Pawel Kisielewski
Varian Ayers & Gary Knisely
Rosemary Leith
Kathryn Ludlow
Emma Marsh
Barbara Minto

Gavin & Ann Neath
William Plapinger & Cassie Murray*
Mark Robinson
Paul & Jill Ruddock
William & Hilary Russell
Jenny Sheridan
Anthony Simpson & Susan Boster
Brian Smith
Carl & Martha Tack
Katherine & Michael Yates

BOUNDARY-BREAKERS
John and Annoushka Ayton
Katie Bradford
Tim Fosberry
Edna & Peter Goldstein
Sue & Don Guiney
Rosanna Laurence
David & Elaine Potter Charitable Foundation

MOVER-SHAKERS
Anonymous
Dianne & Michael Bienes*
Lois Cox
Cas & Philip Donald
Duncan Matthews QC
Ian & Carol Sellars
Jan & Michael Topham

HISTORY-MAKERS
Jack & Linda Keenan*
Miles Morland

MAJOR DONORS
Daniel & Joanna Friel
Deborah & Stephen Marquardt
Lady Sainsbury of Turville
NoraLee & Jon Sedmak*

*Supporters of the American Friends of the Royal Court

FOR THE ROYAL COURT

A Miracle

Characters

Val Metcalf, *sixty-three. Mother of Sandra, John and Ian. Grandmother of Amy. Great-grandmother of Cara.*

Amy Aston, *nineteen. Granddaughter of Val. Mother of Cara. Trained as a hairdresser. Works in a chicken-nugget factory.*

Gary Trudgill, *nineteen. Has been away in the army for two years, training to be a carpenter and joiner.*

Rob Trudgill, *forty-eight. Gary's father. A pig farmer who has recently lost his farm due to foot-and-mouth and financial difficulties.*

Cara, *Amy's baby, just under a year old.*

Setting

A village in Norfolk, May 2008.

Prologue

Val *is in her kitchen talking to a baby in a pram.*

Val   Pity my ma never lived to see you, Carabelle. She'd a' told ya some stories. There ent much use for reality out here, but I could tell ya a few truths. I could tell ya a tale of witches burning at the stake. Of boys catching their feet on shopping trolleys. A tale of kids playing adults. Of girls who say, 'I don't worry about HIV, I only sleep with boys from Suffolk.' I could sing ya a song of welly boots and blood, knitting needles and castor oil. 'At would have be pigs that scream, a girl who can't feed herself, a boy who knows only how to destroy things. A miracle baby. And a flatness that consumes us.

Scene One

Evening. **Val** *alone onstage with baby. Bags of fruit and vegetables and other market buys on the table and floor.*

A door slams. **Val** *quickly kisses baby and takes her offstage.*

Amy *enters. She wears jeans, vest top and a bomber jacket, and carries a small handbag.*

Amy   A'right, Nan. (*Shouts.*) Nan?

Val (*off*)   Shhh.

She enters.

How was work?

Amy   Oh, beautiful. Think I've still got bits of chicken skin under my nails.

Val   Thought you'd wear gloves.

Amy   We do. I just mean . . . It feel like I can't get rid of the skin, the smell – it's gross.

Val   You don't have to do it, you know.

Pause. **Amy** *continues washing her hands.*

Val   Cara's in the bedroom, sleepin'.

Amy   Right.

Amy *slumps at the table.*

Val   The two of us had fun today.

Amy *picks up a fork from the table.*

Val   Went to the WI market. Poor turnout.

Amy   Cara must a' been gutted.

Val   But guess who we did see?

Amy   Uh . . . Mum?

She starts messing around with the fork, pressing it into her arm.

Val   No. That wouldn't be much of a game, would it?

Amy   Yeah, as if Mum'd be seen dead at the WI.

Val   That old friend of yours. Good-lookin' boy.

Amy   At the Womens's Institute?

Val   Naw, at the bakery.

Amy   Don't sound like anyone I know.

Val   I used to clean fer his mum.

Amy   You used to clean fer a lot of people's mums. If you don't know his name how am I supposed to guess?

Val *takes the fork from her.*

Val   Had that farm, went to join the army –

Amy   You're jokin me – Gary Trudgill?

Val   Back, en' he? Coming round as it happen, to put up some shelves. He's on leave, I'm employing him fer a change. How the mighty have fallen, eh?

Amy   What shelves? When?

Val   He's now on his way, love. Just gotta call in on a friend first, he said. Shepherd's pie saved for ya.

Amy   But Cara's here, Nan. I'll have to take her to mine, won't I, if he's coming? What shelves?

Val   To yours? What you wanna take her there for?

Amy   Putting up shelves will make a lot of noise.

Val   You're being silly, child. Eat.

Amy   I know you, Nan.

Val *pushes leftover pie towards her.*

Amy (*pushing it away*)   I'm good, ta.

Silence as **Val** *puts away the shopping, puts the kettle on.*

Amy *slumps in a chair at the kitchen table.*

Knock at the door.

Val   Oh, bloody forgot, din' I?

She starts putting on her coat.

Amy   What are you doing?

Val   Said I'd take shepherd's pie round to ol' Cecil.

Amy   You can't / leave me to –

Val   Won't be long, love, don't forget to check Cara.

Amy   Course I bloody –

Val *goes to leave.*

Amy   Like ya forget, Nan.

Val *opens door.*

Gary (*off*)   A'right, Mrs Metcalf?

Val (*off*)   Gary love, forgot to feed poor Cecil. Won't be a minute. Amy's in, just go on through. She's looking forward to seeing ya.

Amy   Bitch.

Gary *enters in uniform, carrying a large travel bag.*

Gary   A'right, Amy?

Amy   A'right, Gary.

Gary   Long time no see.

Pause.

Looking well.

Pause.

Did ya nan say she'd seen me?

Amy   Mentioned it.

Gary   Want me to put up some shelves.

Amy   Do she?

Gary   Only just got back.

Pause.

Called round Johnny Leigh's, but his mum say he live up
Norwich now. So.

Pause.

Might have to come back another time, actually, when I've got
me tools.

Pause.

Thought I may be of some use. Since I'm back. From army.

Amy   That what they learn you in the army? Putting up
shelves?

Gary   Learn you killing mostly. But I know carpentry.

Silence.

Amy   Remember Year Six primary? You cried cos that plant
died?

Gary   I was ten.

Amy   What ya doing here?

Gary   Told ya – shelves. Just doin' a recce. en' I?

Amy   I mean, back here. Are ya injured?

Gary   Got R and R, en' I? Rest and relaxation.

Amy   How long you back for?

Gary   'S up to me. Just rechargin' the batteries – you still go up Hollywood's?

Amy   Sometimes. It got shit, just fifteen-year-olds now.

Gary   Well, that were us, weren't it? We should go, old times' sake.

Amy   You and me?

Gary   Yeah, yeah, why not? 'At'll be a laugh. Get someone to sort us out beforehand, see if –

The sound of a baby crying. He jumps.

Shit, what the fuck's that?

Amy   It's a baby. Crying.

Gary   Shouldn't you go and –

Amy   Yeah. Hang on.

She sees to **Cara** *and returns.*

Amy   'At's done. What / were –

Gary   Sorry 'bout before. I don't normally swear so much, specially not in front of . . . I mean, I'm all about respect, you know?

Amy   Sure.

Gary   So, whose baby is it?

Pause.

Amy   Mine.

Gary   Gotta say, and I know it's – but you don't look like someone who's just had a baby.

Amy   I ha'n't just had her. She's a year, almost.

Pause.

You wanna meet her?

Gary   Uh, yeah.

Amy *runs off.* **Gary** *looks uncomfortable.* **Amy** *comes in with sleeping* **Cara** *in her arms.*

Amy   Here. She's called Cara.

Gary   Hello.

Pause.

Amy   She don't speak yet.

Gary   She's beautiful.

Amy   D'ya think?

Gary   You make me laugh, you do. Don't every mother think her baby's beautiful?

Amy   Yeah, course. I know she is.

Silence for a moment as **Amy** *struggles a bit with* **Cara**.

Amy   What were ya saying?

Gary   When?

Amy   Before.

Gary   Before . . .

Amy   Before she started cryin'.

Gary   Was I? I can't –

Val (*off*)   Told ya I wouldn't be long and that was even with ol' Cecil chatterin' on –

She enters, a bit out of breath.

What you doin girl, you'll wake 'er. Always fussin', this one, Gary. Gotta just let 'er be . . .

She takes **Cara** *from* **Amy**.

Val   There now, my Carabelle.

Scene Two

Rob *is outside on the farm.* **Gary** *enters. Watches him silently for a bit.*

Gary   A'right, Dad?

Rob   A'right, Gary buh [*boy*].

Pause.

Gary   Good to see ya.

Rob   Y'mum thought y'were gonna be back few hour ago.

Gary   I was. Bumped into an old friend up town, got dragged in for a cuppa tea.

Pause.

Mum say dinner's ready.

Rob   Right. Picked a great time to take holiday, din' ya?

Gary   Yeah. Ent that much choice, though. So.

Rob   An' ya mum say ya back fer a while?

Gary   'At's right. Maybe.

Silence.

Ya comin' in then?

Rob   Sin the new house?

Gary   Just downstairs.

Rob   'At's a shithole.

Gary   'S all right. Bit small, en it?

Pause.

Food's up, Dad.

Rob   Whole place is a shithole. Adam McCabe don't know what he's doin.

Gary   McCabe? That make me laugh – some city boy?

Rob   Got some romantic notion about farming, ha'n't he?

Gary   But he listen to you, right? Lucky he's got someone here who actually know how things go.

Rob   Won't ya think about what ya sayin', buh? This was my farm, an' now I'm an *employee*? Nothin's the same as before, buh. People that used to have respect are runnin' round like they own the place, laughin' at us –

Gary   'At's been bad for everyone, ha'n't it? / You'll get through.

Rob   I've lost the most.

Gary   But din' we survive the worst bit, when everyone else was closin' down? I dun' get . . . What happen –

Rob   Well. 'At's over. Belong to another man now, dun' it?

Gary   You could get somewhere else. Smaller.

Rob   You dun' know the way it work, son. Ya never have.

Pause.

Gary   Anyway. Mum say dinner's ready, so . . .

Rob   I'll be there in a minute.

Pause. **Gary** *stays.*

Rob   Tell 'er. I'm now comin'.

Gary *leaves.*

Scene Three

The following afternoon. The park outside **Val***'s house.*

Amy *is sitting on a roundabout. She rocks* **Cara** *in a pram beside her.*

Amy   If I knew a song I'd sing it to ya. Bet Nan know a lullaby or two. Bet Nan make ya stop when you start crying. Bet Nan talk to you about the future and how it's gonna be. How it's gonna be OK, cos we all love ya so much. Are ya listenin', Cara?

She shakes pram.

Cara, sweet?

Shakes pram bit more violently.

Gary *enters.*

Gary   Y'right, girls?

Looks in pram.

Hello, sleepy. Just passing.

Amy   Really? (*To* **Cara***.*) Remember Gary? He live down the way. Well, he used to, now he's just here for his holidays. His parents own a farm.

Gary   Not any more. Anyway, I ent got nothing to do with that.

Amy   Pig farm, ent it, Gary? Ent no shame in it, they're loaded. But Gary don' work there.

Gary   Not for all the tea in China, darlin'.

Amy   Don't reckon she's ever heard 'all the tea in China'.

Gary   So we're teaching 'er somethin'. Gary don't wanna deal with pig shit, not for love nor money.

Amy   In fact, Gary say stuff shovelling pig shit for a game of soldiers.

Pause.

Don't change much, do it?

Gary Don' it? You got a baby. Gyppos from the caravans over the marshes roamin' all over town.

Amy Only they en' gyppos. They're from all over, I work with some of 'em at the nugget place.

Gary Bet ya get all the gossip, factory floor.

Amy Nah. Most of 'em don't even know English. Nan used to get more when she worked at St John's. Y'know 'bout Ben Newsom? He ent so good. Dead, in fact. He were swimmin' in the mere with Jimmy Allen and caught his foot on one of them shopping trolleys at the bottom and . . . Know who's a mystery, though? Who even Nan can't find the whereabouts of? Dean Adams.

Gary The King of Fish 'n' Chips?

Amy His family still own the chippy but he no longer do the books. And apparently in six months he's been spotted just twice, once in the Marlowe in Boxton wearing a suit and once driving through Norton at high speed in a BMW.

Pause.

Gary Crazy.

Pause.

Amy Yeah. Not exactly gossip . . .

Gary You still connected?

Amy What? No. No.

Gary An' Johnny's up Norwich. What 'bout Bobby?

Amy Bobby give up. Anyhow, he's in Australia.

Gary And Bobby's . . . Is Bobby Cara's dad?

Amy No. Well, sort of.

Gary Sort of?

Amy Technically, I suppose. But he's in Australia, travellin' an' all that.

Gary   Don't he wanna spend time with his daughter?

Amy   Don' s'pose so. Well, Cara weren't born when he left.

Gary   How could he not wanna see this little one? I like what you're doin'. You're a strong lady, Amy. Single mothers, I really respect them. Good girl.

Pause.

So, you and Bobby never speak, email?

Amy   No.

Gary   OK. Maybe Tash can sort me out.

Scene Four

Rob *outside on farm.* **Gary** *enters.*

Gary   Sorry. With a friend.

Rob   Dun' wanna be too friendly with anyone around here.

Gary   Know me. Friendly with everyone, en' I?

Rob   One of them girls, was it? From school?

Gary   Sort of.

Rob   Always round here. So many of 'em.

Gary   Remember Amy Aston? Val's granddaughter. Val Metcalf, who clean for us?

Rob   I know, I know, I know 'er. Forgot her name's all. Val. Bitch.

Gary   She's all right –

Rob   Ha'n't worked here fer ten month, have she? She was one of them. Laughin' at me all the while, like she knew this were gonna happen.

Gary   She never say, are ya sure –

Rob   Tell ya what buh, stick around here fer a couple o' years, then ya can tell me what I can an' can't be sure of. Ya can do better than that girl, buh. You was always aimin' higher, remember?

Pause.

Gary   I know what I'm doin'.

Rob   What, just messin', son?

Gary   Yeah, just messin'.

Rob   I was thinkin' 'bout what ya said, 'bout tryin' a' get somewhere new. The money fer this place en' gonna go far, but . . . 'at would be tough. And would be a risk, no denying. But 'at might just be possible.

Gary   Course 'at is. You weren't made to take orders. 'At don't make sense, how 'at happen.

Pause.

Ya can't have this nobody who knows nothin' about farming tellin' ya what to do.

Rob   'At'll be a lot of work.

Pause.

Gary   But I can help.

Rob   Can ya?

Gary   Yeah. Yeah. Looks like they're closin' our unit.

Pause.

Yeah, I'll be based back over in Thetford, won't I? So I'll be about to lend a hand.

Pause.

Mum said ya never had lunch, so busy. What ya want me to do then?

Rob   Gotta load this stuff, en' we?

Gary   Right.

Scene Five

Amy's *flat. Evening.*

Amy *and* **Gary** *enter with chips in paper.*

Gary   So this is Amy's World.

Amy   Needs all o' five seconds to take in.

Gary   There are plus points though.

Amy   Yeah?

Gary   I reckon you could lie in, cook breakfast and have a shower all at the same time.

Amy   Yeah, toast get a bit soggy though.

They laugh.

Plates. We need plates, dun' we?

She goes about looking.

Gary   Not much room for Cara's stuff.

Pause.

Amy   No, she don't spend much time here.

Gary   She's at ya nan's a lot?

Pause.

Amy   Yeah, I work at the nugget factory and try to keep this place. I do see Cara, but she mainly live with Nan. 'At's what they worked out. Kinship placement, until I decide . . . until . . .

Gary   Can't ya mum help out?

Amy   I can't find . . . Nah. She just got rid o' me and Darren. She go out more than me nowadays. Be mad to want another kid livin' with her, specially one that ent her own.

Pause.

Just, don't always feel like she's mine either. An' cos she's a baby, they could get her a nice family, with jobs an' everythin' quite easy.

Pause.

Have I freaked you out? Shit, I'm totally freakin' you out.

Gary   It take a bit more than that nowadays, darlin'.

Amy   Cos you've seen the world? Dunno why you'd come back.

Gary   There's things ya miss, you know?

Pause.

Now I'm back, it seem like another world out there.

Amy   Only it ent. It's the same.

Gary   But being here, with you, I forget that. I forget what it's like.

They kiss. **Amy** *pulls away.*

Gary   I meant it when I said I admire ya.

Amy   But I'm a horrible person. I'm a mess. I understand if you're like, 'Look, I'm now goin', yeah.'

Gary   Why would I do that?

Amy   Cos I'm horrible and mean and a bit psycho?

Gary   Y'know I don't think that. Y'know I think the opposite of that.

They kiss.

Amy   Chips'll be gettin' –

Gary   Fuck the chips.

Amy   Yeah, fuck 'em.

Scene Six

The following morning. **Amy**'s *flat.*

Morning.

Gary *is lying back in bed smoking.*

Amy *enters with a bowl and mug.*

Gary   What've we got?

Amy   Cheerios and hot chocolate. Managed to pick up then?

Gary   Helen Beake, would ya reckon.

Passes her the joint.

Cheerios and hot chocolate, don't get much better than that, do it?

Silence as **Gary** *eats and* **Amy** *smokes. She passes it back and he tries to hand her the bowl of cereal.*

Amy   I'm good, ta.

Silence.

How many people did ya kill?

Gary   It ent really like that.

Amy   How?

Gary   What?

Amy   How ent it like that?

Gary   Well, you don't keep count, do ya?

Amy   I would.

Gary   Well, you don't know cos you ent fuckin' been there.

Amy   Sorry.

Gary   Just, everyone here always ask, 'How many d'ya shoot? How many d'ya kill?' But it ent – I mean, hardly anyone do. I could though. I know how to.

Amy   Oh.

Silence.

Gary   In case you were wonderin', I've only ever done that with four people.

Amy   Sex?

Gary   Sex without . . .

Amy   Oh, fine. Long as you're careful. (*Pause.*) I'm all spinny.

Gary   What would you do, if anything were possible? In an ideal world?

Amy   I'd . . . work in a salon.

Gary   A hairdresser's?

Amy   Yeah, trained as a hairdresser, din' I? Was workin' at Freya's in Norton. It was a good job. But then, Cara.

Gary   'At's a fantasy. You don't have to be a normal hairdresser in a salon, you can own it.

Amy   OK, I'd own a salon and call it 'Amy's'. And I'd have a car with the number plate AMY. And a huge house, in Norwich though –

Gary   What about Cara?

Amy   Well, Cara ent there, if this is a fantasy. I mean, she ent born yet, not until . . . She don't exist yet. I'd wanna be settled in my house first. You go now.

Gary   I'd leave. I'd just leave here, the army. Go somewhere good, like Brighton.

Amy   Always thought it were weird, you bein' in army. Bein' told what to do all day – at school ya just did what ya liked.

Gary   Still do what I like. I wan'ed to come back so I did, din' I?

Pause.

We could go to Brighton, couldn't we?

Amy   Together?

Gary   Could go fer a coupla days. My cousin Kelly? She's studying there. It's better than Norwich, or Southwold, or whatever. You've got the sea, the arcades, decent shops.

Amy   'At sound great. Don't go back.

Scene Seven

Val's *kitchen.*

Val *is stewing plums and listening to the radio.*

Cara *is asleep in her pram.*

Amy *enters.*

Amy   Nan, I need ya help.

Val   Hi, love, didn't know you were coming.

Amy   Didn't know I needed an appointment.

Val   Course you don't. We coulda been out.

Amy   But you're not. Hello, Cara.

Rocks her in her pram.

I wanted a favour.

Val   Careful there.

Amy   I wan' a' do some proper cooking. En' like Mum taught us, all she do is from frozen. (*To* **Cara**.) A'right, beautiful? Gary say she's beautiful!

Val   Bumped into that couple from the factory earlier, stick out like a sore thumb, they do. Asked after ya. Said you were off sick yesterday?

Amy   Kristi and Neville?

Val   White girl and coloured man?

Amy That's them. I'm entertaining tomorra night, I need a recipe, Nan.

Val Were ya ill?

Amy Tummy ache. I was thinking toad-in-the-hole and Lemon Delicious.

Val Bit tricky.

Amy Gotta start somewhere, ha'n't I?

Val Who you entertainin' then?

Amy You know, that Gary?

Val Oh, that Gary.

Amy Shut up. I should learn to cook right for Cara anyway.

Val Yeah, we want this one to know the evil of food that look nothing like what it is, dun' we?

Amy I'll have to go up town for food so y' wanna write me a list?

Val I'll make it if ya want? Make sure it's perfect then. Fer Gary.

Amy Reckon I can do it.

Val OK then, s'pose it don't have to be perfect, do it?

Amy I could take Cara fer a walk while you make it?

Val Why don't you make the most of ya day off? You get the ingredients, I'll cook and mind Cara.

Amy I don't mind taking her out though, Nan.

Val She's now settled. And you know how she get irritable being moved around this time a day.

Amy Do she? Well. She'll be gettin' an excitin' trip out soon though. To Brighton. Me an' Gary are gonna take 'er. I think she'll like it. 'At's supposed to be amazin' –

Val Say who?

Amy Say Gary. But I heard that already too.

Val And how long Gary gonna be about for?

Amy Let's just say it's lookin' like longer than he first thought.

Val Must be nice, havin' a friend about?

Amy And ya know, Nan, he's different, he's got a proper job, he's sort of gentlemanly –

Val Funny. Didn't think the army encouraged gentlemen.

Amy You liked him enough the other day, din' ya?

Pause.

Val It's just, I dun' want ya to get carried away. There's somethin' about that boy that's –

Amy Do ya sense it? Like one o' them fortune witches? They'll be takin' you down Mellis an' drownin' you or somethin' soon. I'll go up town then?

Val A'right then, love.

Amy I won't take Cara, 'at's so annoyin' with the buggy. Be nice fer her to go to Brighton fer a few days, to see a bit o' the world, don't ya think? Don't ya think, Nan?

Pause.

Val Yeah, yeah, I'm sure 'at would. Are you goin' fer them ingredients or have we gotta wait in all day?

Amy A'right, dun' get tetchy. Is ya great-nan in a bad mood today, Cara? Silly Nana. I'll be quick then.

Scene Eight

Amy's *flat. Night-time.*

Amy *and* **Gary** *in bed.*

Gary *has just woken from a nightmare.*

Amy   What's wrong? D'ya want water?

Gary   I went into the Co-op earlier and I started sweatin' cos I ha'n't got a gun.

Amy   Was it the Lemon Delicious? D'ya think / it gave ya dreams?

Gary   Cos the last time I saw someone like that, I needed a gun. Behind the counter –

Amy   Oh. Yeah, Ammar. Don't worry, he's all right.

Gary   What?

Amy   That bloke you saw, he's OK, I know him.

Gary   You know him?

Amy   Yeah, it's fine. He's nice, I promise. Go to sleep.

Scene Nine

Outside on the farm.

Rob   Told McCabe what I think of him today.

Gary   He'll be buggered if y'walk, won't he? 'At's stupid, he own the place an' he don't know shit. An' you . . . I just dun' get how ya can have a farm one minute an' –

Rob   There's a plot. Smallholdin', down Lodger's Road. One that used to belong to Terry Akers.

Gary   I know it.

Rob   It's small.

Gary   'At would be a start though.

Rob   I dunno, buh. I'd have to do it with no borrowin' an' not much money to start with. Maybe 'at's just all over. 'At's all over fer me now.

Gary   Ya can't just give up though, Dad. You'd be unbeatable if ya made a success of Akers' place.

Rob   Well . . . if ya endin' up in Thetford, then I suppose 'at might work. 'At could be the two of us runnin' it? Would only take ya forty minutes from Thetford to here in the evenin'. And in the mornin', you would be startin' at about five. Train ya up. We wouldn't get a wage so much, at first. That'd be the only way, I reckon. An' in a year an' a bit, when ya done ya army time, I'll think about makin' ya my partner.

Pause.

Most farmers' sons . . . Aaron, what do he do? Jamie Pett? Andy Hurst's son? They're all workin' their guts out on the family business. To keep it afloat in time like this.

Pause.

Ya mum act so proud when ya went off. Tellin' all the ladies about where y' were trainin', places ya might go. Now ya back, 'at's like ya runnin' off at every moment. Spendin' ya time knockin' around with some scally girl ya wunt touch with a bargepole when y' at school. She'll have that kid callin' ya Dad, just you see!

Pause.

I dunno. 'At's just idea. 'At might not work. But I reckon, with the two of us −

Gary   'At's worth a try.

Rob   'At's right, buh. 'At's right.

Scene Ten

Amy's *kitchen. Early hours of the morning.*

Amy *and* **Gary** *enter. Drunk.*

Amy   Do ya feel old?

Gary   I'm glad I'm not fifteen any more, and that I got outta this shithole, that's what I feel.

Amy *puts the kettle on.*

Gary   Y'know, this place really is a dump.

Silence.

There's cobwebs everywhere. Don' ya want somethin' better fer yerself? You wanna talk to my mum cos she's really good a' – I can see a spider, Amy.

Amy   I like that spider.

Silence as **Amy** *makes a cup of tea and he watches her, slowly getting more angry.*

Gary   Did you ever think? I could have a gun. I could have brought a gun back with me.

Pause.

I know how to use one.

Pause.

Amy.

Amy   I know ya do.

Gary   I know how to shoot someone dead. To shoot a man dead.

Pause.

Or a woman.

Pause.

Or a child. A baby.

Pause.

I could shoot a man or woman or baby dead. Or all three.

Pause.

Amy?

Amy   You must be very proud.

Gary   I am actually, yeah. I'm a very fucking proud person actually. Not that I get much fer it. Come back here, minor celebrity about Mum's friends for a few days, then no one want to know. No one care. I've got skills. I'm trained. Not like them round here, workin' in fuckin' . . .

Silence.

You can be really rude, you know. I know –

Amy   How to kill someone? Except you ha'n't ever done it, have ya?

He hits her, she falls on the floor.

Gary   Get up – as if that hurt.

She sits up.

I think I caught your eye. I'll fix it.

He moves towards her.

Amy   It's fine.

Gary *sits next to her on floor. He takes a packet of powder out of his pocket, spoons some out and snorts it.*

You want? It's OK, it's for horses.

She takes it.

Amy   Whatever.

Pause.

I'll do whatever you want.

He reaches for her.

Blackout.

Scene Eleven

Later that evening. **Amy**'s *flat.* **Amy** *and* **Gary** *still on the kitchen floor.* **Amy** *cradles* **Gary**.

Amy   I wish I could chase them bad dreams away, but all I know is sad stories and boring things.

Gary   Tell me boring things.

Amy   Well, I'll tell ya about my day?

Gary   OK.

Amy   Fer about nine and a half hours today I watched a pulp of half-frozen skin being minced up and squeezed through a tube and pressed into nasty little nugget shapes. That skin look like pale, pimply raw bits of baby. It go past me on a belt and's lowered into pouring batter. Then I put these bits of fucked-up skin into plastic bags and cardboard boxes sayin' Tesco or Somerfield or whatever.

Gary   I ent eatin' nuggets again.

Amy   That's pretty much every day fer me, normally.

Gary   'At'll be different soon though. We'll have a nice break in Brighton.

Amy   An' Kelly'll be all right with Cara comin'?

Gary   Yeah, surely. An' if she en', we might have to leave her behind, this time. Dun' worry though, 'at'll be fine.

Scene Twelve

Val's *kitchen.* **Cara** *in pram.* **Gary** *enters.*

Gary   Hello? Anyone home?

Pause. He notices **Cara**.

Gary   Hello, Cara. A'right?

Pause.

Where's your gran then? Has she left you all alone? Has she been a bad grandma and left Cara by herself?

Pause.

Wish I were you, Cara. When ya sad ya cry, dun' ya?

Stands watching her.

You awake, Cara?

Reaches into pram.

Val (*off*)   Amy? Hello . . .

Gary   A'right, Mrs Metcalf?

Val *enters.*

Val   What ya doin?

Gary   Come a' see Amy, en' I?

Val   She en' here. I en' seen her fer days. As well you know.

Gary   Reckon she must be at work then.

Val   Good enough for ya now, is she? Wouldn't have a bar of her before.

Gary   At school?

Val   Funny how things change, en' it?

Gary   En' my fault if −

Val   Missed her meetin' with the social worker yesterday.

Gary   Never mentioned it. She must've forgot.

Val   Ha'n't missed one before.

Pause.

If you feel any tiny little bit of something for that girl, ya need to just let her be. She need to be here, with me and her daughter.

Gary   Do she? Seem like she prefer bein' about me.

Val   You're a novelty is all.

Gary   Reckon I'll wait till Amy tell me that, thanks all the same.

Pause.

'At's great, how ya look out fer Amy. Pity ya en' as caring to the others around ya.

Val   Excuse me?

Gary   Dad reckon you were just waitin' fer him to fail, an now 'at seem 'at's true. 'At's disgraceful.

Val   What? I spent years cleaning up their rubbish.

Gary   You were paid fer it.

Val   Yes, love, it was a job, wouldn't have done it fer free.

Gary   But ya were there fer years. It was more than a job, right, ya knew them like family.

Pause.

My dad put a gun to his head.

Val   That were after I left, Gary. The swine fever were the start, weren't it? Faulkard's farm were infected, so fer five months ya dad couldn't move the pigs. They couldn't sell the ones that were reaching full weight and couldn't stop the sows from giving birth. You should know all this, buh.

Gary   Times got a bit hard so you all jumped ship?

Val   It were traumatisin' just doin' the cleanin', but we stuck it out. There were three hundred pigs squashed in them tiny pens. Fightin', screamin', tearin' each other apart. Ya could feel death all around. Kept all the horror away from you an' ya mum, up in the Big House, o' course. Don't reckon I once saw you on the farm, did I?

Gary   I'm here now, ent I? 'At dun' make sense, he get through foot-an'-mouth – and then *this*?

Val   Called in a loan, din' they? An' ya dad couldn't . . . He had t' pull himself back up, buy more an' more flash stuff, keep up appearances, an' I reckon that's how he lost the place. We knew they wouldn't be able to pay us all fer much longer. They were clearly in trouble. We all got our worries, buh, but they ent *my* family.

Pause.

'At'll be shock, 's all. He loved that farm. 'At'll be post-traumatic stress. Amy have it, after Cara.

Gary   After having a baby?

Val   Birth's brutal. Blood, shit, the lot. I bet we saw as much blood and guts around here as you lot did out there. But I bet you never paid us much thought.

Gary   Not much chance of that, with Mum writin' all the while. Had to stop callin' cos she sounded so . . . Then she start writin', and I can't take seein' her words, and the heat – Over there it feel like standing up close to the exhaust on a tractor, 'at's so hot. And I can't believe what she's sayin' about him, cos / he's always been so –

Val   So ya back fer ya dad? Compassionate leave?

Gary   An' then I start makin' . . . Start doin' stupid . . . My mind's not on the job is 'at. And his face haunt me all the while.

Pause.

Sick leave.

Val   How long ya back for?

Gary   Two weeks, so ya dun' need to panic. Two weeks to sort my head out.

Val   'At might be a bit difficult doin' et round here, buh.

Gary   En' my fault everyone wan' a bit o' me. I never said nothin'. I never agreed to be this fer them. 'At's better bein' here an' gettin' abuse than bein' stuck at that cottage.

Val   Just don't forget the rest of us have been here all the
while. And will stay here when you go.

Scene Thirteen

Amy *and* **Gary** *at the park, lying down.*

Amy   I'm in a hole. I'm in a hole . . .

Gary   Just relax.

Amy   Take it eeeasy! (*As sung by Mika.*)

Gary   Idiot.

Amy   What're we doin' here again?

Silence.

Gary   Amy? I've scraped dead bodies off the ground with a
shovel, put 'em in bin bags and left 'em by the side of the road.

Amy   'At's in the past. We gotta forget about that stuff.

Pause.

Know those pregnancy advice manuals? I bought them and
did the opposite. Did everythin' in my power not to have Cara.
I was on twelve coffees a day, pub every other night, three
curries a week, even got gym membership.

Gary   You're jokin' me?

Amy   Can't ya tell I've toned up?

Gary   There's a war going on and ya wouldn't know it cos
it's somewhere else. But it's also everywhere I go. I take it with
me.

Amy   Just . . . don't think about it. We'll be OK. We'll keep
safe.

Gary   I ent sure. / I ent –

Amy   There's this couple at the nugget factory, Kristi and
Neville. I met her at the lockers. She's from Moldova and he's

from Namibia. She used to live in a flat over in Lowestoft, one-
bedroom flat with eight others. She were makin' sixteen
pounds a week, after gangmaster took money for rent and
travel and papers, cos she's here illegal. But Neville's legal an'
he sees this happenin' and he tells Kristi she being taken for a
fool and helps her escape this gangmaster. So the gangmaster
is now after her, claiming she owe him money and every so
often Neville has to take him on. Neville is this big bloke. And
Kristi and Neville have this home and . . . this language. Their
own language, it's sort of Moldovan-English sign language, I
suppose. But for months that's how they communicated, across
the factory floor. Even now, though her English is really good,
they use it.

Silence.

It's like, they've made this new life for themselves. Out of all
the crap. Out of everythin' they've seen and that's been done
to them, and all of the people that don't want them around,
somethin' good has come – they've found each other. All they
need is each other. They've made this little space on the earth
and they belong there.

Silence.

Ya reckon we could be like that? One day?

Gary Yeah. 'At'll be us against the world.

He takes a packet out of his pocket.

More?

Scene Fourteen

Val's *kitchen.*

Amy *enters. She carries a pink bag and is a bit of a mess.*

Amy A'right, Nan? (*Shouts.*) Nan?

Val (*off*) Shhhh.

Val *enters. She takes a look at* **Amy**.

Val   Dinner?

Amy   I'm good, ta.

Val   'I'm good, ta.' Always 'good, ta'. You are, are ya? Cos ya look a state.

Amy   I'm sorry I missed the meetin'.

Val   Ya can't keep choppin' and changin', Amy.

Amy   I know. I know that, dun' I? Got Cara something yesterday. Extra pay cos of last Sunday.

Val   That's nice.

Amy *carefully takes a dress out of the pink bag.*

Amy   Wanna see, Nan?

Val *stares at the dress.*

Amy   It's from Michael's, in town. It's a boutique. Worth the money cos of the quality.

Pause.

Val   Cara's ten months, Amy.

Amy   I know, dun' I?

Val   What age do it say inside?

Pause.

Amy   Eighteen. Thought she were big fer her age though.

Val   Not that big.

Amy   Well, I guess / she can grow . . .

Val   It'll drown her.

Pause. **Amy** *starts to put the dress away.*

Val   Silly to waste nice material though. I could adapt it, make her a nice little top?

Amy   If ya want.

Pause.

Can Cara stay at mine tonight, Nan?

Val   Not tonight, love, not at such / short notice.

Amy   But they recommend it, dun' they? That we become part of each other's routine an' that?

Val   Not before ya ready.

Amy   An' if I'm takin' her to Brighton soon it'll get her used to havin' me there at night.

Val   When ya reckon ya goin' on this Brighton trip then?

Amy   I dunno. Couple of weeks. Gotta book a few days off, it en' definite.

Val   Gary'll be back in the army by then, won't he?

Amy   No. He's got ages.

Val   Do he? That's not what –

Amy   I'm sorry about the meetin'. Really. 'At wun' happen again –

Val   'At better not. You can't just drop her cos ya found a new friend.

Amy   I wouldn't do that, Nan. 'At's more time I wanna spend with her, not less. I'm sayin' I want her to stay, en' I?

Val   So you can practise for Brighton?

Amy   Not just that. To . . . get to know her better. Just me and her. That's what I care about: me and Cara.

Val   That's how 'at should be.

Amy   See, ya even think that y'self.

Val   There won't be no visitors?

Pause.

Amy   No.

Val   Y' can't take 'er if ya gonna be havin' people round.

Amy   People?

Val   Cos that's the condition.

Amy   I en' interested in anyone else.

Val   Bring her back here in the morning before work.

Amy   I will, 'at'll be first thing, I'm on an early.

Val   All right. All right then. But if she seem tired or –

Amy   She won't. I'll read her one book, an' that'll be it. Thanks. Thanks, Nan.

Scene Fifteen

Amy's *flat.*

Amy *is standing by the door.*

Gary *is outside.*

Amy   I can't let you in.

Gary (*off*)   What?

Amy   Cara's here.

Gary   So?

Amy   So you're drunk.

Pause.

Gary   Let me in.

Amy   I can't.

Gary   She won't see me. She wouldn't understand anyway.

Amy   You can't be drunk around a baby.

Gary   You can.

Amy   No you can't, it's –

Gary   OK. Nice. You're being all motherly. / Let me in.

Amy   I am?

Gary   Amy . . . You get time to think in the army. Get so as ya want someone to write to. Ya want something delicate and precious. That's you.

Amy   Shhh, it's embarrassing. (*Giggles.*) The neighbours.

Gary   I don't care who hears.

Amy   Look, we'll talk in the morning, yeah?

Gary   I need to come in. I think you're so . . . petite. Amy. (*Shouts.*) Amy? Y'can't leave me out here.

Amy   Hush. I'm now opening the door.

She does so, and **Gary** *enters with beers and candles in a bag and flowers with some earth still attached to them.*

Amy   Hello.

Gary   Don't do that again. I wanna see the baby.

Amy   She's asleep.

Gary *leaves the kitchen. Sets up candles in the living room.*

Amy *goes about making some toast.*

Amy   Gary?

Gary *enters, swigging a beer and still carrying the flowers.*

Amy   Toast?

Gary *drops the bag of beers and the flowers, jumps animal-like on* **Amy** *and pushes her onto table, kissing her, pulling at her.*

Amy (*after a few seconds*)   Hang on. Hang on.

Pause.

Gary   What? Fuck.

Amy   Just . . .

She pulls him back to her, trying to make him slower, but **Gary** *pays no attention. After a few seconds, he is done. He backs off. Lights a joint, drinks his beer.*

Amy *gets herself together uneasily.*

Silence.

Cara *starts crying.*

Amy   I should / go and . . .

Gary   These are for you.

Hands her the flowers, which he has tried to resurrect.

Amy   Thanks.

Gary   Amy, I wan'ed talk to ya.

Cara *continues to cry.*

Gary   That OK?

Amy   Yeah, course.

Gary   I wan'ed to say, I think we should have the trip to Brighton next week.

Amy   OK. I'll have to make somethin' up to tell the factory then. An' ask Nan, she only just let me take Cara / fer one night.

Gary   'At's just, I can't be about here no more.

Amy   'At'll be fine. I'll do 'at tomorrow. Are ya parents drivin' ya mad? Imagine how much Cara'll / love the beach! Can ya smell . . .

Gary   D'ya reckon Cara should definitely come? 'At'll be the toast.

Amy   I never burnt it.

Opens the kitchen door.

Shit. Shit.

Gary   Shit. The candles.

Amy   Cara. Cara's in –

Gary   I'll get her, call –

He shoves his phone at **Amy**.

Gary   Get out, Amy!

Amy   My baby! There's a fire –

Scene Sixteen

Val's *kitchen.*

Amy *paces the floor.*

Val *enters.*

Amy   Is she OK? Nan?

Val *nods.*

Amy   Omigod. (*She cries.*) Thank God. Thank God. I made some peppermint creams for her, fer when she get out.

Val *slaps* **Amy** *across the face.*

Amy (*sobbing*)   You shoulda let me come, Nan. You shoulda let me.

Pause.

I'm her mum.

Val *slaps her again.*

Val   Then act like it. Peppermint creams are pure sugar. You've lost all right to see that child.

Amy   But I'm her mum. Don't ya want her to see her mum?

Val   I don't want that boy anywhere / near –

Amy   It was an accident. Gary did bring her out, Nan.

Val   Promise me. Promise you won't be spending any more time with him. You won't let him near Cara.

Amy   It was candles. He was being romantic.

Val   Promise. You've been lucky with social services. It only take one word from me. They'll take her away.

Amy   I promise. I promise.

Pause.

Nan. I do – love her, you know.

Val   Course ya do, Amy, you're her mother. But what good's love if it dun't protect her?

Amy   We'll tell 'em, Nan. I want her. I wanna be her mum an' keep her safe. I'll get better at it. I promise.

Scene Seventeen

Outside on the farm.

Val   A'right, Rob.

Rob   What? Oh. A'right.

Val   Well. 'At's bin a long while.

Rob   Kirsty's inside, I think.

Val   Come to see you, din I? It was Kirsty said I'd find ya out here.

Rob   Right.

Val   How ya doin?

Rob   Grand. Grand. Can I help ya?

Val   'At's like goin' back in time, being back here. Nothin' change.

Pause.

Kirsty's made the cottage nice. Always good at that sort a thing, weren't she?

Rob   Are ya laughing at me?

Val   No. No, buh. Why'd I do that?

Pause.

I mean, it weren't like you shoved it in our faces when ya had money, was et? Weren't like you were laughing at us. Revvin' ya engines. Takin' ya holidays. Cos then I'd reason to laugh, wouldn't I?

Rob   If there's nothin' I can help ya with, ya should be goin'.

Val   You wanna tell ya boy, stop hanging round my granddaughter, promising her goodness knows what.

Rob   Ah. Well, ya can't tell Gary nothin', see. That's the thing about my son, always been his own man, en' 'e?

Val   That right? When 'e was a kid an' you used to beat the living daylights out of him, he din' look so much like he were his own boy – looked very much like he were your boy.

Rob   Like I said, if there's nothin' I can help ya with –

Val   Don' s'pose you seem such a big man to 'em now.

Rob   Y' need to watch ya mouth there.

Val   No, not now he knows his big, strong dad tried to blow his brains out.

Pause.

Rob   What?

Val   An' ya know, I really wouldn't care, only it's lookin' like a case of like father, like son – an' I don't want him promisin' my granddaughter the earth when he's only back fer a couple of weeks.

Rob   You dunno what ya talkin about, woman. Gary's helpin' me with a new farm.

Val   You old bloody fool. The army own him now, not you. He's on sick leave cos his poor little brain can't cope with the fact that his ol' man is a mess. He en' gonna help you with nothin'. Ask him, and when ya do, make sure to tell him to stay the hell away from my girls.

Scene Eighteen

Val's *kitchen.* **Amy** *alone with* **Cara**.

Amy *is trying to measure* **Cara** *up for a top out of the too-big dress.*

Cara *stirs.*

Amy   A'right there, Cara? A'right there, Little-Fingers?

Cara *starts to cry.*

Amy   A'right, Tiny-Nose? Hold still for me, can ya, Diddle-Ears?

Pause. **Cara** *still crying.*

Amy   Shall we read a story before Nan get back? A nice happy-ending story?

Cara *still crying*

Amy   Come on, Cara.

Still **Cara** *cries.*

Amy *walks away a moment. Walks back. Watches* **Cara** *cry. She picks* **Cara** *up.*

Amy   Come on, come on then, you.

Car *cries.* **Amy** *holds her.*

Scene Nineteen

Gary *outside on the farm, smoking.*

Rob *enters. Charges at* **Gary**, *trying to hit him.* **Gary** *pushes him off without much effort.*

Gary   What ya doing?

Rob   Val Metcalf say ya on sick leave.

Pause.

Gary   Well, ya don' wanna listen to everythin' / she say.

Rob Are ya, buh?

Pause.

Gary Yeah.

Rob An' ya only back fer two weeks?

Gary Yeah.

Rob An' ya always knew? Even when ya go, "At'll be fine, we'll set up a smallholdin'"? You always knew ya were only about fer two weeks?

Gary Yeah. But 'at's true, they are pullin' troops out. I could be back soon. I could be stationed at Thetford. I din' want ya to give up.

Pause.

I just wan'ed to give ya some sort of hope fer the future.

Rob *launches himself at* **Gary** *again, this time swiping his face.* **Gary** *pushes him to the ground.*

Gary I'm not a kid any more, see.

Rob Patronising little bastard, en' ya? Shoulda known, cos you never did give a damn about the farm.

Gary Course I –

Rob Although, you were always happy to march around it as a boy. Like ya owned the place. Showin' off to ya mates. Chattin' about this tractor, that one. The number of staff.

Gary It ent –

Rob I know how it is, buh. You don't need to tell me what it ent. I see it clear as day. Ya think ya too good. I blame myself. Bringin' ya up to think you were somethin' better than most the folk round here. Indulgin' ya dreams of seein' the world. All so ya could go from here an' –

Gary It en' news that I'm a disappointment to ya. Dun' ya reckon I've always known it? Least 'at's now mutual. When I first went out there, 'at was lonely an' 'at was borin' an' ya can't exactly call anyone a friend. But I thought, ya all right though, ya know who y'are. Ya come from someone strong. Y'come from a man who worked hard to get what he got. Ya come from a man who wan'd ya to take into school the best bag, the best bike. Even if I weren't fussed about it myself. A man who got ya a car at fifteen, so ya could drive ya mates around an empty field. Never even driven that car on the road, have I?

Pause.

You're the reason I wan'ed to leave here for ever, and the reason I wan'ed to come back an' go down the pub an' show 'em what I'm made of.

Pause.

An' then, I find, that man tried to top himself.

Pause.

Ya think Mum never tell me? You think she's not pickin' up that phone the moment it happen?

Rob   Nothin' *happened*.

Gary   Ya took the gun.

Rob   Ya mum gettin' hysterical over nothin' is all.

Gary   But ya took the gun?

Rob   Up to the back field and back.

Gary   With intent. Ya took it with *intent*.

Rob   Think you're a fuckin' lawyer? Think ya see how it is but ya don't. I went up the fields with a gun. Yes. To think. Yes. To. Consider my options, ya might say. Ya reckon I'd even fail at pointing a gun at my head and pullin' the trigger? As if you got what it take to run a place like this, buh. You chose to spend ya time as a yes-man, din' ya? Ya lie to y'self like ya lie to us all. But I got ya number, buh, an' I can see what ya doin'. No one make another person get sick. If you en' man enough

fer the job you chose to do, dun' go blamin' me. If you en'
man enough –

Gary *goes to leave.*

Rob   'At's right, buh, you run.

Scene Twenty

Val's *kitchen.*

Gary, *with bruised eye, sitting on a kitchen surface, kicking legs against
cupboard, or some other restless, destructive activity.*

Amy *enters.*

Amy   Jesus. How'd you get in?

Gary   No one lock their door round here.

Amy   Nan do. What happened to ya eye?

Gary   An' if they do they leave the key in the flowerpot in
the back garden. Accident.

Pause.

Look.

Takes keys from pocket.

Dad's car keys. Let's go to Brighton.

Pause.

Amy   Gary, did ya set fire to my flat on purpose?

Gary   Course I never, what –

Amy   Sorry.

Gary   Fuck sake, Amy.

Amy   Sorry. Nan's takin' Cara fer a check-up. I promised . . .
They'll be back soon. Can I come an' see ya later?

Gary   Not really. I'm off.

Amy   What?

Gary   I'm goin' to Brighton.

Amy   I thought –

Gary   Well, I gotta go now. I can't be about here no more.

Pause.

Amy   Right.

Gary   I want ya to come with me, Amy. Not fer a holiday though, fer a fresh start. For ever.

Amy   What?

Gary   Kelly's found a place. A studio flat. They say we can move in when we like.

Amy   Serious? For good?

Gary   I got to. 'At's either that, or go back to the army in two days.

Amy   Two? But ya –

Gary   I know. I got et wrong, I . . . made a mistake about that.

Amy   Thought it was up to you.

Gary   Can ya just listen a moment?

Amy   Thought you had as long as ya wan'ed.

Gary   Ya bein' thick, Amy. Ya really reckon they just go, 'Yeah yeah, take a holiday long as ya want'?

Amy   So, just dun' go back. Stay here, we'll save –

Gary   Listen, you fuckin'– I can't stay about here. I'm supposed to be back in two days. If they find me – well, I can't let 'em, if I go AWOL.

Amy   So. Ya lied?

Pause.

Gary   Dun' be so – Ya bein' ignorant, Amy. Ya dunno how it work.

Pause.

I'm doin' this fer you, y'know. Riskin'. So we can have a better life.

Pause.

I dun' wanna go without ya. Do you understand?

She nods.

I'm gonna do carpentry. There's more job opportunities there. Kelly say there's lots o' salons, they're well into all that. Maybe we could even buy a place. 'At's a buyer's market, en' it?

Amy   But. We dun' have any money, Gary. Can't we wait? Save up a bit –

Gary   No, I'm goin' tonight. I've gotta. 'S up to you, if you dun' wan' –

Amy   'At's not that, it's . . . I only just told Nan I'm gonna be a proper mum to Cara. I can't. I dunno if I can do that somewhere new.

Gary   Dun' that tell ya somethin'? You've had ya doubts in the past. An' she'll always know that, wun' she? She'll always feel it, that ya din' wan' 'er. She dun' wan' a mother who en' sure.

Pause.

You're beautiful, Amy. Cara's hardly a clean slate, is she? She'll always be a reminder of . . . somethin' else.

Amy   You said Cara's beautiful.

Gary   She is. I like Cara. I like babies. An' we'll have 'em eventually, I'm sure. When the time's right.

Amy   You . . . rescued her from that fire. You brought her out.

Gary   Ya said y'self, Cara can get a nice family right now. One that's ready fer her. One that's been waitin' fer her an' can give her a decorated room an' all the love she need. She deserve a good family.

Pause.

'At's what ya said ya wan'ed, in an ideal world: no baby.

Amy   But it en' an ideal world.

Gary   We're two of a kind, ya know. You wanna escape this. I dun' wanna go back to the army. 'At could be amazin'. Think about 'at. There won't be no pig farms −

Amy   Or chicken nuggets −

Gary   Or baby's nappies.

Pause.

Or baby's nappies.

Val (*off, from outside*)   Amy? Could ya get the door . . . ?

Gary   Why shouldn't we have the lives we want? We deserve et.

Amy   You gotta go.

Gary   'At's gotta be tonight, Amy. I'm gonna call by Helen Beake, then I'm gonna give ya a bell, an' you can meet me at the park. OK?

Val *enters with* **Cara** *in buggy.*

Gary   A'right, Mrs Metcalf?

Val   Wha' −

Gary   Dun' fret, I'm now goin'. (*To* **Amy**.) I'll bell ya.

He exits.

Val   Amy.

Amy   Sorry. He only just now come over.

Val   Least he'll be goin' away soon enough.

Pause.

Amy   Yeah.

Cara *stirs.*

Val   Cara's all fine, ya'll be pleased to hear.

Pause.

Amy   Good. 'At's good.

Val   Dun' s'pose ya managed to make a start on dinner?

Cara *starts crying.*

Amy   Sorry.

Val   I'll learn ya how to make my hotpot tonight if ya want?

Pause.

Cara *is still crying.*

Amy   Shall I put Cara down?

Val   She'll be difficult to settle right now. I'll do it if ya –

Amy   I wanna.

Val   OK. Have a try.

Amy *exits with a still-crying* **Cara**.

Val *starts cooking.*

Cara *still crying offstage.*

Amy *enters with a bag and her coat on.*

Amy   I'm off, Nan.

Val   What?

Amy   To Brighton. To live. With Gary. Enough o' this shit.

Val   That what ya call ya daughter now, is it?

Amy   Yeah. Cara, the factory, makin' rent. You, Mum, feelin' the guilt. All these months I've been trying, and it shouldn't be so hard. It's nature, ent it? But I don't know if I feel . . . much. I can't feel. I can't. She's yours, Nan. Always has been, really, ha'n't she?

Val   Dun' be –

Amy   Gary's found a nice flat. We're gonna live there. I'm
not comin' back. He's leavin' the army. For me. He's done that,
fer me.

Val   He's on sick leave. Do 'e seem like a well man to you,
Amy? Do you know what they do if ya leave before ya s'posed
to?

Amy   Don't care. 'At's gotta be better 'n here. Got what ya
wan'ed, ha'n't ya? Me an' Gary, you an' Cara.

Val   This en' what I wan'ed.

Amy   But you set us up. You brought him back here.

Val   I thought he'd take ya to the pictures. Get yer a drink.
Drive ya 'bout town. Thought ya needed cheerin' up. Snappin'
out of it.

Amy   I did. I did need that. An' I've been snapped out of it,
en' I? I feel now, Nan. I feel alive. An' it ent cos of my
daughter. 'At's cos o' him. En' Cara that make me happy, 'at's
Gary.

Val   An' what about that little mite in there? What about her
happiness?

Amy   She's a baby, Nan, she don't know. You look after her.
I'm goin' with Gary.

Val   They'd never let me. I'm sixty-three. I live alone. I . . .
They'd never let me.

Pause.

Amy   Then. You'll have to sort something out.

Val   You know Sandra can't take her.

Amy   Mum's got more sense. Nan? Mum barely even know
Cara. There's been no room for her, with all your messing.

Val   Maybe she got the right idea. Thankless job anyway,
bringin' up kids. They never remember all you do fer 'em.

Pause.

Amy   Well, Cara won't have nothin' to remember then.

Val   You can't expect everythin' to come quick, Amy. En' nothin' wrong with strugglin'. Everybody do.

Amy   But I don't wanna struggle. I've had enough of strugglin'. I don't wanna get by, I wanna live.

Val   Listen. They'll take her away –

Amy   Not my problem.

Val   From everyone she know . . .

Pause.

Amy   I don't care.

Val   Is that what you want? Put her in a strange place.

Amy   Shut up. Fuckin' shut up.

Val   We can sort –

Amy   You just don't give up, do ya?

Val   That's what you do, when you love someone –

Amy*'s phone rings.*

Amy   I got a chance here. With Gary. / A new start.

Val   You don't give up. You stick with them. Look at her, Amy. She look like you. Her bird-face.

Amy*'s phone is still ringing.*

Amy   Shit, Nan. I got a chance and I en' gonna blow it.

Val   You don't leave, when ya care for 'em –

Amy*'s phone stops ringing.*

Amy   Dun' ya see? I ha'n't cared for her. I ha'n't loved her right. This ent the only time I've rejected her, Nan. I rejected her when she were inside me too. I wanted her out so badly. And when I think what I did. It's a miracle. Course, I woulda got it done by a doctor. Only, he's bin my doctor since I was a baby, en' he? An' I'd have to pass em in the street. An' I'm not fourteen any more, ya know. If Dee and Clare can have babies when we're in Year Ten, and Mum had Darren at sixteen, why can't I have one a' nineteen? Why can't I?

Val   Amy –

Amy   That's what you're supposed to think about your child, ent it, it's a miracle. Only she really is, cos I tried fuckin' everything for it not to be this way. All I wanted was to scream and shout and be sick and tear my hair and scratch out my eyes and I didn't though, I didn't. But what I did was every fuckin' trick in the book. Fuckin' housewives' stories. I drank stuff down, I stuffed stuff up. Burnt my skin in the bath –

Val   I dun' believe ya.

Amy   It's true, even the stuff that din' happen. Cos I woulda done it, if I had the energy. If I weren't so. Dead inside. And all everyone do is assume. Assume I'm happy. Assume I'll cope. Assume I'll love my child. But I can't and I don't want her and that make me . . . Don't know what that make me. Maybe there ent even a word for that. I dun' deserve her, Nan. She really is a miracle, see.

Val   'At's OK. 'At's OK.

Amy's *phone rings again.*

Blackout.

Scene Twenty-One

Park. Morning. Two days later.

Amy *sitting on the roundabout outside* **Val**'s *house,* **Cara** *in a pram beside her.*

Gary *enters with travel bag from Scene One.*

Amy   A'right, Gary?

Gary   A'right. A'right, Cara?

Amy   So. Ya off then?

Gary   Solved the mystery of Dean Adams. Did I tell ya? Met him up the town. He's working as a gangmaster's heavy – how he can afford all that stuff.

Amy   Always knew he were a wanker.

Gary   More than keeps the wolf from the door though, dun' it? He offered me a job for when I come back, said my trainin' might be useful.

Silence.

AWOL's more trouble than 'at's worth. Brighton'd be a shithole just like here.

Silence.

Amy   Think ya'll come back?

Gary   Dun' reckon. I mean, war's rubbish, but it's better than here. Round here, no one care what go on over there.

Silence.

'At's sick. 'At's sick, what's goin' on here. 'At's sick, what ya bringing ya daughter into.

Silence.

Amy   We must look like a family.

Gary   What?

Amy   From the outside, we must look like a family.

Amy *pushes off on the roundabout.*